Author Claudine Destino

P.O. Box 769122

Roswell, GA 30076

kitchendiva2003@yahoo.com

www.kitchendivadesigns.com

Copyright © 2011

ISBN-10: 0-9728462-1-2

ISBN-13: 978-0-9728462-1-9

WIMMER

COOKBOOKS

ConsolidatedGraphics

1-800-548-2537

Table of Contents

Cooking Tips

- ◆ **<u>Anchovy Paste</u>:** Found in a tube next to the canned anchovies in specialty shops and grocery stores. Use ½ teaspoon as a quick substitute for 1 anchovy filet. Refrigerate the open tube up to 6 months unless it develops off flavors or becomes moldy then discard immediately.

- ◆ **<u>Apple Corer/Slicer</u>:** One of the best gadgets in my kitchen. In one swift action it removes the core and cuts the apple into 6 – 8 equal slices. A great time-saving tool for making pies, desserts, salads or makes a quick snack for the kids.

- ◆ **<u>Asparagus</u>** is plentiful during its peak season February through June. Choose fresh, firm stalks, with tightly closed caps. To remove tough ends, bend each spear until it snaps. For thicker stalks, peel the outer layer with a vegetable peeler to the tender middle. To store: put ½-inch water in a tall, narrow jar or glass. Cut off ½-inch from the butt end of the asparagus and place in the jar. Make a tent with plastic wrap or plastic bag and refrigerate. Will keep fresh up to 1 week if the water is changed daily.

- **<u>Avocados</u>** that are ripe are firm but yield to gentle pressure. If avocados are bright green, store on the countertop or in a paper bag until they turn a brownish/black color. When ripe, store in the refrigerator up to 1 week. To peel, make a cut through the skin down to the pit from top to bottom. Twist the halves apart and remove pit by tapping it sharply with the blade of the knife. Twist the pit to remove from the flesh. Cut the flesh into a dice or slices with the tip of a knife while still in the skin. Scoop out the flesh with a spoon and gently separate with your fingers. The flesh of avocados can be stored in the freezer by mashing with 2 tablespoons lemon juice.

- **<u>Bacon:</u>**

  1. For easy removal of bacon slices, roll the whole package into a cylinder beginning with the short end; unroll and pieces will "peel" off each other better. If you only use bacon occasionally, separate into individual slices, wrap each piece in plastic wrap, and place wrapped pieces in a zip top freezer bag. Store in the freezer up to 3 months. When a recipe calls for a few slices of bacon, remove only as many as needed.

◆ **<u>Bacon</u>:**

2. To make **<u>bacon</u>** bits: remove desired number of slices from package in one piece or layer several pieces together. Chop or cut all slices at once into small pieces with kitchen scissors or a knife. Fry over medium heat, separating pieces as they cook. Cook until crisp and golden brown.
3. There are 16 – 20 slices/pound of regular sliced bacon; thin sliced=28 – 35/pound; thick sliced=12 – 15/pound.

◆ **<u>Bain-marie</u>** (water bath): Used to cook delicate foods such as puddings, custards, mousses, some cheesecakes or any food requiring moist, indirect heat. To make your own, place the dish containing the food into a larger baking pan and pour boiling water about halfway up the sides of the dish containing the food. To prevent burns, it is safer to add boiling water to the second pan after the pans have been put in the oven. Pour the water into the second pan and then carefully slide the rack back into the oven and proceed with baking. This method promotes even cooking and prevent scorching.

- **<u>Baking bags</u>** are used to bake foods in the oven creating an airtight environment keeping foods moist and easy cleanup. They can be found in the grocery aisle with aluminum foil and plastic wrap.

- **<u>Baking powder</u>** still active? To test, drop ½ teaspoon into a glass of warm water; if it fizzes it is o.k. to use. Always measure and level off the measuring spoon. Never put a wet spoon into the container; it will deactivate the whole can.

- **<u>Baking soda:</u>** To test for freshness, mix ¼ teaspoon baking soda into ¼ cup vinegar; if it bubbles like crazy, it is fresh. Never cook with baking soda after it has been used as a refrigerator freshener.

- **<u>Balsamic vinegar</u>** is a dark-aged Italian vinegar, fermented 10 – 15 years, and has a slightly pungent-sweet taste. Buy the best you can afford. Most balsamic vinegars sold in grocery stores are just caramel-colored vinegars.

- **<u>Bay leaf</u>:** A firm leaf of the evergreen bay laurel tree. Can be used dried or fresh. Imparts a lemon-nutmeg flavor to long-simmered soups, stews, vegetables, fish and meats. Remove from the cooked dish before serving because it can be a choking hazard if swallowed. As a general rule, use 1 bay leaf per quart of liquid.

- **<u>Bell pepper</u>:** Comes in a variety of colors: red, yellow, orange, purple, and brown, but the most common is bright green. One of the "dirty dozen" vegetables that retains pesticide residue. Buying **<u>organic</u>** is highly recommended. Store in the refrigerator up to two weeks. To slice or chop, first cut in half through the stem. Grasp the stem including the inside membrane and bend until it snaps out. Repeat with the other half. Scrape the remaining membrane and remove the seeds. Slices easier with the skin side resting on the cutting board.

- **<u>Boursin cheese</u>** is a buttery, triple cream cheese, flavored with herbs, garlic and/or pepper. Look for it in the specialty cheese section.

- Tough cuts of meat (chuck and shoulder roasts and brisket) need to cook by **braising**—cooking in a small amount of liquid at a low temperature for a long time to tenderize.

- ## **Breadcrumbs:**

  1. Save all your dried, leftover bread (baguettes, sandwich bread, bagels, crackers, rolls, etc.) and put into the bowl of your food processor or blender and pulse until you have fine crumbs. Or rub dried bread on a grater, catching the crumbs in a bowl. Store crumbs in a zip top plastic bag or tightly sealed container in the freezer and use as your recipe directs. Homemade breadcrumbs tastes superior and fresher than store prepackaged.

  2. Two slices of bread=1 cup fresh breadcrumbs. Put bread in the bowl of an electric blender or food processor and pulse until finely grated.

◆ **<u>Broccoli</u>** that is freshest will have firm stalks with tightly bunched heads. The florets should be a blue-green color. If broccoli shows signs of the buds beginning to turn yellow, it is past its prime. Refrigerate broccoli in a plastic bag up to 4 days. If broccoli becomes limp, trim the bottom off the stem and stand in a container of cool water. Refrigerate overnight. 1 pound raw broccoli will yield 5 cups; 1 pound cooked will yield 3 cups.

◆ **<u>Brown sugar:</u>** To store, place opened bag of sugar in another plastic bag. Remove as much air as possible and tightly close, or empty into a tightly covered container. To keep sugar soft, place a marshmallow on top and seal tight. If sugar has hardened, soften by placing in a microwave-safe dish, covering tightly and microwave on high power for about 30 seconds. Generally, light-brown or dark-brown sugar can be interchanged for each other. When measuring, always lightly pack sugar in measuring cup.

- To **soften butter** or margarine: place in a microwave-safe dish and microwave on 20% power 1 minute.

- No **Buttermilk**? To make a good substitute, stir 1-tablespoon vinegar or lemon juice into enough milk to measure 1 cup and let sit 5 minutes.

- **Canola oil:** A cooking oil low in saturated fats containing omega-3 fatty acids that is believed to lower cholesterol and triglycerides. Made from rapeseeds, its bland flavor is suitable for cooking and salad dressings.

- **Cantaloupe** when ripe should have a sweet, melon aroma. Choose a melon with a soft stem end and raised netting with a yellow/tan undertone. Avoid shriveled, green or rock-hard melons.

- **Capers:** The tiny, unopened flower bud of the caper bush. They have a sharp, salty-sour taste cured in salty white vinegar. Find them in the pickle aisle of your local grocery store.

◆ **Cast-iron cookware:** The original nonstick cooking pans. This heavy cookware, made from iron or cast iron, distributes heat evenly and retains high temperatures. Some are coated with enamel, but the old-fashioned pans must be "seasoned" before using to prevent sticking. To season: scrub with soap and hot water. Dry thoroughly and rub all surfaces with oil or shortening. Place in a 250° oven for 15 minutes; remove from oven and wipe away any excess grease. Return to oven and bake 1½ – 2 more hours (or turn oven off and let sit overnight). Repeat the greasing and baking procedure 2 – 3 more times until the pan is dark with a nice sheen. Really, the best way to season is continued use and gentle cleaning. Always dry after washing, because water is the enemy of these pans. Unfortunately, cast iron can never be put in the dishwasher.

◆ **Cheesecakes** need to cool slowly after baking to prevent cracking. Some recipes suggest leaving the oven door slightly opened after baking and the heat turned off. A great dessert for making ahead because they need to be chilled thoroughly before serving. Cheesecakes can be frozen tightly covered up to 1 month. Thaw in the refrigerator.

- **Chèvre** (pronounced SHEV ruh) is a deliciously tart, goat cheese, ranging in textures from moist and creamy to dry and semi-firm, sold in different shapes such as logs or cones. It can be plain or coated with herbs, crushed pepper or edible ash. Usually found with the specialty cheeses. Wrap any leftover chèvre in plastic and store in the refrigerator up to 2 weeks.

- To **cook chicken** for use in any recipe requiring cooked chicken: sprinkle lemon pepper (or season with salt and pepper) on chicken breasts (boneless or rib-in) and place inside a baking bag (smaller version of the kind used to bake turkeys at Thanksgiving) or tightly seal in aluminum foil. Put on a baking sheet in a 350° oven about 1 hour. Remove from oven and cool in the bag. Remove and chop chicken as recipe directs. Reserve any accumulated juices in the cooking bag by pouring into a container and storing in the refrigerator up to 2 days or 3 months in the freezer. These juices are "liquid gold". Use in any recipe that requires chicken broth or bouillon.

◆ **Chicken breasts** (boneless, skinless) should be even thickness to prevent some parts from drying out before the whole breast is cooked through. Pound each breast in a large plastic bag or between 2 sheets of plastic wrap until ½-inch even thickness. Or carefully slice the entire breast lengthwise with a sharp knife to make two chicken breasts.

◆ To **debone chicken breast:** slip a thin knife or fingers under the breastbones and pull away from the flesh. Slit the flesh around the larger bones with a knife and carefully lift out bone avoiding taking too much flesh with the bone.

◆ **Chicken tenders:** the long, side muscle on the breast. It is not totally necessary remove the white tendon but if you prefer: grasp the end of the tendon with a paper towel. Pull the tendon towards you while holding the chicken with the edge of a knife.

◆ <u>Chicken or meat</u>

1. Should be removed from refrigerator 1 hour before cooking or grilling to allow it to come to room temperature so that it will cook more evenly.

2. Both will slice easier and thinner when partially frozen. Slice chicken the length of the breast and all meat across the grain.

◆ <u>**Chives**</u> are a member of the onion family but have a much milder flavor. Snip fresh chives with kitchen scissors to desired length. Store rinsed and dried fresh chives in a plastic bag in the refrigerator up to 1 week wrapped in a dry paper towel.

- **<u>Chocolate:</u>** To melt, chop chocolate bars into small pieces. **1)** Place uncovered in a microwave-safe dish and microwave on high power (100%); stir every 20 seconds. Chocolate can be removed from oven while still lumpy; the heat of the dish and the chocolate will continue to melt lumps. Be careful not to overheat; chocolate burns at a low temperature; Or **2)** Put chocolate pieces into the top of a double boiler and place over hot water. Stir occasionally until chocolate is melted. (**<u>Do not</u>** let any water droplets or steam mix with chocolate or it will become a hardened, grainy mass. If this happens, work in or stir a small amount of melted vegetable shortening, 1 teaspoon at a time, until chocolate returns to a liquid state.)

- **<u>Chocolate:</u>** To grate or shave, rub chocolate bar over a coarse grater or shave with a vegetable peeler to make curls.

- **Chocolate dessert cups:** melt chocolate chips. Coat the bottom and 3-inches up the insides of a small paper cup or cupcake liner with the melted chocolate. Cool until set. Repeat. Refrigerate until completely hardened. Carefully peel away the paper from the chocolate. Trim the top if edges are ragged.

- **Coconut:** To toast, place on a large cookie sheet. Bake at 350° until lightly toasted, about 12 minutes, stirring frequently.

- **Coconut milk and red curry paste** can be found in the Oriental section of most grocery stores.

- **Cookie crumbs: 1)** Place cookies in a plastic bag (don't close all the way). Smash with a meat pounder or rolling pin, Or **2)** place cookies in a food processor or blender and process until fine crumbs.

- **<u>Cream (heavy or whipping)</u>:**

  1. Bowl and beaters should be very cold before whipping because colder cream whips up easier and faster.

  2. If you over whip cream (it separates into solids and liquids), gently fold in a few tablespoons of milk or more cream. To stabilize whipped cream (to keep it in soft peaks longer), add 2 tablespoons nonfat dry milk or 1 teaspoon cornstarch to every cup of heavy cream before you whip it.

  3. Half-and-half is 10 – 12% butterfat (milk fat); light cream is 18 – 30% butterfat; light whipping cream is 30 – 36% butterfat; heavy or whipping cream is 36 – 40% butterfat.

  4. Heavy cream or whipping cream can be used interchangeably.

- To **<u>soften cream cheese</u>:** unwrap and place on a microwave-safe dish. Microwave 30 seconds.

◆ **Cream sherry or dry sherry:** Buy in the wine section of the grocery store or specialty shop.

◆ **Crème fraîche:** A soured cream containing about 28% butterfat but is thicker, and less sour than sour cream. Find it in the dairy section of the grocery stores. **1)** To make a good substitute mix ¼ cup buttermilk into 1 cup cream in a jar or container. Lightly cover jar and set in a warm place for about 24 – 36 hours, until mixture is thickened. Cover and chill (it will thicken more as it gets cold like soft yogurt). Whipped crème fraîche will keep whipped in the refrigerator up to a week or several hours at room temperature. **2)** Or mix 1 cup whipping cream with ½ cup sour cream. To make a delicious, tart whipped cream, whip until soft peaks form.

- **<u>Croutons:</u>** To make homemade, slice slightly stale, hearty French bread into slices. Brush slices with extra virgin olive oil or vegetable oil (for garlic croutons add 1 clove crushed garlic to the oil). Stack a few slices on top of each other and cut into cubes with a serrated knife. Put in a single layer on a baking sheet and bake in a 350° oven 10 – 15 minutes or until crunchy, stirring midway of the baking time. Cool completely and store in an airtight container.

- **<u>Cracker crumbs:</u>** To make, place crackers in a plastic bag and finely crush with a rolling pin, wine bottle, meat pounder or with hands. Or put crackers in the bowl of a food processor or blender and pulse until crackers are crushed. Make cracker crumbs from leftover crackers and store extra in the refrigerator or freezer.

- **<u>Dale's Steak Seasoning®</u>** is a soy sauce based sauce found in most grocery stores next to other steak or barbecue sauces.

- If you do not have a **double boiler**, you can easily make one by nestling a smaller saucepan in a larger one or use any heat-proof bowl that will sit securely on top of a saucepan without touching the boiling water. The heat of the steam, generated by the boiling water, cooks the food.

- Fresh **eggplant** has a smooth, glossy, dark purple skin. Buy eggplant that feels heavy, has a green stem, and unblemished skin. Store in the refrigerator up to 2 days.

- To cook hard-boiled **eggs:** place eggs in a saucepan in a single layer and cover with cold water to come 1 inch above eggs. Bring to a boil, immediately cover. Remove from heat and let sit covered 15 minutes. Remove from hot water and immerse in cold water to cool fast. Tap eggs all around to crack the shell and peel under cold running water.

◆ **Eggs** separate easier when cold. Break egg into a funnel or into your fingers over a first bowl. The white will easily slip into the bowl and the yolk will remain in the funnel (or your fingers) as long as it is not broken. Transfer white to a separate, second bowl and the yolk to a third bowl. Using three bowls keeps an accidentally broken yolk from contaminating the whites already separated. Whites with even a small amount of yolk will not whip up to soft peaks. Repeat with remaining eggs.

◆ **1.** Add a dash of salt to left over **egg yolks** and store in the freezer (1 month) or refrigerator (1 day). Use in custards or add to scrambled eggs.

2. Egg whites can be refrigerated 4 days. Freeze leftover **egg whites** individually in an ice cube tray. When frozen remove from tray and place in a plastic bag. Thaw whites in the refrigerator when a recipe calls for egg whites.

- ## **Eggs:**
    1. For best results, all ingredients for baking should be room temperature.
       To remove the refrigerator chill, put unbroken eggs (in their shells) in a zip top bag and immerse into hot tap water; let sit for a few minutes while assembling other ingredients.

    2. 4 whole extra-large eggs=1 cup; 5 whole large eggs=1 cup;
       5 whole medium eggs=1 cup; 6 whole small eggs=1 cup

    3. 6 extra-large egg whites=1 cup; 7 large egg whites=1 cup;
       8 medium whites=1 cup; 9 small whites=1 cup

- **Fresh Fish** should be odor-free. Fish filets should lay flat and look moist. Whole fish should have clear eyes and red gills. Fish is highly perishable and should be cooked the day of purchase. At most, fish can be purchased the day before but should be kept extra cold. Store in a plastic bag surrounded by ice packs in the refrigerator to keep fish at its maximum freshness. Serve a 6 – 8 ounce filet or 8-ounce fish steak per person.

- Instead of sifting, stir **flour** with a spoon in the storage container until light and separated. Spoon into a graduated, dry-ingredient measuring cup (nesting cups) and level off with a knife or straight edge (never pack down).

- To make **self-rising flour**, add 1 teaspoon baking powder and ¼ teaspoon salt to every cup of flour; mixing thoroughly.

- To **fold** ingredients together: insert large rubber spatula in the center of the mix; drag it across the bottom and then up the sides, rotating spatula and bringing some of the bottom of the mix to the top. Keep repeating this movement while turning the bowl to mix from all sides.

- **Fontina** is a buttery-tasting Italian cheese (there are also American and Danish varieties), like a cross between a Swiss cheese and Brie.

- To crush **garlic:** peel off papery skin by whacking clove with the side of a knife; paper should slip right off. Place the clove between two sheets of plastic wrap and smash with a meat pounder or the bottom of a heavy pan until pulverized. Scrape garlic off plastic wrap and use in recipe as directed.

- Fresh **gingerroot:**

  1. Is found crystallized, candied, preserved and pickled (used for sushi).
  2. 1 ounce = 3 tablespoons minced ginger; 1-inch x 1-inch piece = 1 tablespoon minced or grated. Store extra ginger peeled or unpeeled in the freezer in 1-inch slices. While still frozen, grate or cut into small cubes and push through a garlic press. Or cover fresh, peeled ginger with vodka and store in the refrigerator up to 6 months.
  3. To combat nausea make a soothing ginger tea: cut one-half inch piece and remove the peel. Slice into 7 – 10 pieces. Bring 2 cups water to a boil; carefully add the ginger pieces. Lower heat to a simmer and continue simmering about 15 minutes. Strain liquid into serving cups and stir in honey and lemon to taste.

◆ **<u>Gorgonzola cheese</u>** is a semi-soft, bleu veined cheese with a distinctively sharp flavor yet creamy textured. Best substitute: English Stilton.

◆ Fresh **<u>grapes</u>** will cling to their stems if shaken gently. Grapes should be plump and firm and stems should be green and moist-looking. Grapes are covered by a thin layer of dust, dirt and pesticides. To clean: fill a large bowl with cold water and dissolve 1 teaspoon baking soda and 1 teaspoon citric acid (Fruit Fresh® found in the canning aisle). Let grapes sit in this water for a few minutes, then swish around. Rinse thoroughly. Drain on paper towels and allow to air dry. Clean, dry grapes will keep fresh for several days stored in an airtight container in the coldest part of the refrigerator.

- To **grease and flour baking pans:** cover fingers with plastic wrap or a plastic sandwich bag and spread about ½ tablespoon butter or vegetable shortening over the inside baking surface of the pan. Spoon in 1 tablespoon flour, shaking pan to evenly distribute flour. Turn pan up side down and remove excess flour by tapping edge of pan on the counter.

- To substitute **dried herbs** for fresh: a good rule of thumb is to use one-third the amount of dried as fresh (1 teaspoon dried=1 tablespoon fresh). Always crush dried herbs between your fingers before adding them to your recipe for optimum flavor.

- **Herbs (fresh):**
  1. To chop, roll herbs into a tight bundle and finely chop crosswise with a sharp knife. Or snip with kitchen scissors. To prevent fresh basil and tarragon from darkening while cutting, sprinkle with a few drops of vegetable oil.

◆ **<u>Herbs (fresh):</u>**

2. To store (especially parsley or cilantro): wash herbs in plenty of cold water; drain on paper towels. Roll clean, damp herbs in dry paper towels and place in a tightly covered plastic container. Store 1 – 2 weeks in the coldest part of your refrigerator. Basil can be kept fresh for 3 – 4 days with the stems submerged in cool water in a container at room temperature. Refresh water every day.

3. To preserve fresh herbs for winter soups and stews, make herb ice cubes. To preserve the color and flavor, use boiling water (this blanches the herbs). Cool and pour into ice cue trays. When frozen, remove and store in zip top plastic bags.

4. Some herbs, like cilantro keep better when frozen in oil. Chop in the food processor or blender using just enough oil to create a fine purée. Freeze in ice cube trays or plastic bags. Just remember when using frozen herbs in recipes, factor how the extra water or oil will affect the finished recipe. Herbs can be thawed and drained first if necessary.

- Prepared **horseradish** can be found in the dairy case of most grocery stores next to the kosher items. (Don't confuse with horseradish sauce next to the mayonnaise.) Or you can finely grate your own fresh, peeled horseradish root.

- To create an **ice block** for serving and keeping shrimp cold: fill a large, deep rectangular pan one-half full with water. Place on a level surface in the freezer and freeze completely (24 hours). Dampen the top of the block of ice, and decorate the edges with fresh herbs or anything edible. Fill with additional water to secure the decoration. When ready to serve, carefully remove ice block from pan. Place ice block on a larger serving tray or on a rack over a pan to catch the melting ice; arrange shrimp over the top of the ice.

- **<u>Jicama</u>** (pronounced HE-ca-ma) is an edible, starchy root that looks like a large, dry turnip or radish. It has a crispy, crunchy texture that tastes like a cross between an apple (or pear) and a water chestnut. It may be used raw in salads like 'cole slaw' or because it does not turn dark when cut, can be used on veggie trays or it may be baked, boiled, mashed, or fried like potatoes. Use as a substitute for water chestnuts in any recipe. Available year round, select roots that are firm with no blemishes or bruises. Store refrigerated in a plastic bag up to two weeks.

- To squeeze the maximum amount of **<u>juice</u>** from **<u>fresh citrus fruits</u>** (lemons, limes and oranges): heat fruit in the microwave, 20 seconds for 1 fruit, 30 seconds for two and 50 seconds for three or more. (Or let fruit sit in very hot water for a few minutes. Dry fruit thoroughly before squeezing.) Rub fruit between your palms or roll on the counter with gentle pressure. Cut fruit in half. Stick a fork in the middle: rotate fork in one direction and fruit in the opposite direction while gently squeezing. Catch juice in a bowl or measuring cup. Buy fruits that feel heavy for their size with firm, fresh rind. Citrus fruits will keep refrigerated 3 – 4 weeks.

- If a **lid** does not fit snuggly on the pan, cover the pan tightly with aluminum foil and then place the lid over the foil.

- Small bottles (airline serving size—about 3 tablespoons) of **liqueurs** can be purchased at most liquor stores.

- The best kitchen tool to thinly slice potatoes or other vegetables is a **mandolin**. If you don't have one, use a food processor or a very sharp knife. If you slice with a knife, for safety, cut off a thin slice to make a flat surface so that the vegetable will not roll around as you slice.

◆ Ripe **mangoes** should be mostly red and yield to a gentle squeeze.

  1. To ripen: place in a paper bag at room temperature. Once ripe, store in a plastic bag in the refrigerator for several days.

  2. To slice mangoes: Without peeling, stand the mango on its end, with the stem end pointing up. With a sharp knife, cut straight down on one "flat" side, just grazing the pit. Repeat on the other "flat" side. Trim off the remaining flesh from the pit. Carefully score the cut side of the mango halves in a crisscross pattern through the flesh, just down to the peel. Bend the peel back, turning the halves inside out; cubes of fruit will pop out allowing them to be cut off the peel.

◆ **Marshmallows** will keep fresh longer if stored in a tightly sealed plastic bag in the freezer.

- **Marinate** poultry, meat, fish or vegetables in zip top plastic bags, squeezing out as much air as possible and sealing the bag. Place bag in a glass dish or bowl and refrigerate, turning bag several times for even marinating. Remove bag from the refrigerator 1 hour before cook time to bring meat to room temperature. Discard marinade.

- **Madeira** is a sweet, fortified white wine that leaves a rich taste after the alcohol has been cooked off. It blends deliciously with most meats without being too sweet.

- Allow **cooked meat,** no matter what cut or kind, to "rest" 10 – 15 minutes before slicing or carving to allow the juices to settle back into the meat and prevent them from "flooding" out when meat is cut.

- To keep **meringue** from shrinking and weeping, spread over hot filling bringing meringue all the way to the edges making sure it touches the crust all around.

- ◆ Fresh **<u>mozzarella cheese</u>** is a creamy white ball, sometimes called Buffalo mozzarella (if made with buffalo milk), and can be found stored in a brine mixture in some grocery stores or specialty shops.

- ◆ To keep freshly baked **<u>muffins</u>** warm without getting soggy bottoms, tip each muffin on its side in the muffin cups after removing from the oven.

- ◆ **1)** Choose **<u>mushrooms</u>** with the caps closed around the stems, with smooth tops and without blemishes. Exposed black gills are signs of old age. Never immerse mushrooms in water; they will absorb liquid like a sponge. The best way to clean mushrooms is to wipe with a damp paper towel. Store mushrooms in a paper bag in the refrigerator up to 5 days. **2)** One pound mushrooms=5 cups sliced or 2 cups sautéed.

- Freshly grated **<u>nutmeg</u>** has a superior flavor over ground nutmeg found in a can or jar. Whole nutmegs can be located in most spice sections in your local grocery store. Use a very fine grater for best results. Whole nutmegs can be kept indefinitely in a jar in a cool, dark place.

- Toasting **<u>nuts</u>** adds crispness and intensifies the flavor: place in a single layer on a baking sheet or pan. Preheat oven to 350°; place pan in oven and bake 5 – 10 minutes, or until nuts release their aroma, being careful not to burn. A smaller portion of nuts will toast much quicker than a larger amount.

- To chop **<u>nuts:</u>** place ½ to 1 cup nuts in a plastic bag and smash with a meat pounder on a hard surface. Turn bag over and repeat on the other side. Smashing takes a fraction of the time chopping or slicing does.

- **<u>Sesame oil and chili oil</u>** can be found in the Oriental food section of the grocery store or in specialty shops and should be stored in the refrigerator up to 6 months to slow oil from becoming rancid.

- Small bottles of **almond or walnut oil** can be found in the grocery store with the vegetable oils. Nut oils become rancid very quickly; store in the refrigerator up to 6 months.

- **Old Bay® Seasoning** can be found in the spice aisle of the grocery store.

- Avoid canned **olives** if at all possible. Brine-cured olives packed in oil have a superior taste. Some grocery stores or specialty shops offer olives from the deli counter.

- To chop an **onion:** slice off top. Cut the onion in half, down through the root. Peel off outer layer of skin. Cut onion in a crisscross pattern almost down to the root. Turn the onion on its flat side and slice thin or thick, starting at the end opposite the root. By leaving the root end intact, the onion will not fall apart as you slice and you will have perfectly diced onion pieces. Discard root piece.

- To slice an **<u>onion</u>:** cut off top. Cut onion in half through the root. Peel off outer layer of skin. Turn the onion pieces on their flat side and slice thin or thick, starting at the end opposite the root. By leaving the root end intact, the onion will not fall apart as you slice. Discard root piece.

- To section an **<u>orange or grapefruit</u>:** slice off the top and bottom. Stand the fruit on one of the cut ends. Following the contour of the fruit, slice off the peel and all the white pith in thick strips. After all peel has been removed, cut along each side of the membrane and orange section while holding over a bowl to catch the sections and any juice. When all sections have been removed, squeeze all the remaining juice from the membranes into the bowl. Discard membranes.

◆ **__Parchment paper__ 1)** can be purchased in some grocery stores (check near the wax paper and foil) or specialty shops. **2)** Parchment paper (or wax paper) liners for baking pans can be made by placing the desired pan on a sheet of the paper and tracing around the outside of the pan; trim shape with scissors. Cut multiple layers of paper at the same time and store in a large manila envelope for use later. Lining pans with paper almost always guarantees a recipe does not stick to the bottom of the pan.

◆ **__Parmigiano-Reggiano__** (generically **Parmesan** cheese) is a grating cheese (but can also be eaten as a table cheese) made from cow's milk and is aged for 12 – 18 months with nutty, salty, spicy and floral attributes. **__Pecorino Romano__** is a hard grating cheese made from sheep's milk and is sharper, saltier and stronger than Parmesan.

- A ripe **peach** will be a deep golden color with a strong perfumy aroma. For the fullest flavor store peaches (and all fruit with a pit) at room temperature. Only purchase as many as can be eaten in a short amount of time since peaches will over-ripen quickly.

- To speed ripening of **pears,** wrap individually in paper and store in a paper bag at room temperature until they yield to gentle pressure at the stem end.

- To chop **peanuts or almonds:** use a food processor or place ½ to 1 cup nuts in a plastic bag and smash with a meat pounder on a hard surface. Turn bag over and repeat on the other side. Repeat as necessary.

- If possible wear rubber gloves when handling hot **peppers** and refrain from rubbing your eyes. Wash hands thoroughly to remove any juice that can burn your skin.

- **Pico de gallo** is a combination of diced fresh tomatoes, diced onion, chopped jalapeño pepper, and fresh cilantro tossed with a squeeze of lime, a dash of extra virgin olive oil and seasoned with salt and pepper.

- To minimize waste, buy **pineapple juice** for use in recipes in 6-pack, 6-oz cans. Or reserve and freeze the juice from unsweetened, canned pineapple and use in recipes calling for pineapple juice.

- Mini **phyllo shells** can be found in the freezer section of the grocery store next to the phyllo dough and frozen puff pastry.

- A good **substitute for the phyllo shells:** separate 8 flaky, refrigerated biscuits into 4 pieces (for a total of 32) by peeling the layers apart. Press into 1-inch mini muffin tins and bake at 400° for 8 minutes or until golden and set. Proceed as recipe directs.

- There are 6 – 7 tablespoons of **pudding mix** in each 3.4 or 3.9 ounce box.

◆ **Purée** soup in small batches in the blender until smooth. (Caution! Hot soup will explode out of the blender if the container is more than $1/3$ full and the lid is put on too tight.)

◆ **Quinoa** (pronounced KEEN-wah) is a supergrain with more calcium and protein than a quart of milk. Ounce for ounce it has an equal amount of protein as meat, and contains all the amino acids, calcium and iron. It supplies more nutrients necessary for life than any other food and is full of fiber.

◆ Choose **raspberries** that have no visible decay or mold. Store in an airtight container in the refrigerator up to 3 days. Carefully rinse, just before serving. Storing damp berries hastens decay.

◆ **Red curry paste and coconut milk** can be found in the Oriental section of most grocery stores.

◆ To make 2 cups **<u>cooked rice</u>**:

   1. Bring $1\frac{1}{3}$ cups water to a boil; add $\frac{2}{3}$ cup long grain rice. Lower heat, tightly cover and simmer 14 – 18 minutes until all liquid has been absorbed. (1 cup dry rice plus 2 cups liquid will make 3 cups cooked rice.)

   2. Basmati rice has a distinctive, perfumy, nutty flavor and aroma. It is used widely in Indian cuisines and pilafs.

◆ Freshly **<u>roasted red peppers</u>:** heat grill to high heat. Place washed red bell peppers over high heat. Or place peppers on a foil-lined baking sheet and place under the broiler. As peppers blacken, rotate to cook on all sides. Remove from heat and place in a tightly covered bowl 30 minutes. Peel blackened skin, remove seeds and membranes inside by gently scraping. Do not rinse. Doing so will wash away some of the flavor. Use as directed in any recipe.

- **1.** To perk up bottled **salad dressings,** stir in 2 tablespoons freshly squeezed lemon juice and 1 clove crushed garlic.

- **2.** Jam or jelly is a natural thickener in salad dressings that are slightly sweet, allowing for less oil. Substitute any seedless jam or jelly as desired by gently melting in the microwave and adding in place of some of the oil in the dressing recipe.

- To wash and store **salad greens:**

  - **1.** Cut off the stem end from romaine, red leaf, green leaf or iceberg lettuce. Separate leaves and rinse thoroughly with cold water. Shake or spin dry to remove excess water. In a 2-gallon zip top plastic bag, alternate single layers of salad leaves and paper towels. Repeat layers until paper towels surround all the leaves. Remove as much air as possible, close bag and place in the coldest part of the refrigerator (bottom). Salad will stay crisp and ready to eat for up to 1 week.

  - **2.** Or swish leafy greens in a bath of salt water to remove dirt and grit.

  - **3.** Serve 1 – 2 oz. (1 – 2 cups) of salad greens per person.

◆ **Baby salad greens** or **mesclun** is a mix of baby greens usually in a wide range of colors, textures, and tastes. Handle carefully: like all babies they are very delicate. Because they are very perishable, purchase and store no more than one day ahead of serving.

◆ **1.** To toast **sesame seeds:** place in a preheated, dry skillet in a single layer. Shake pan or stir seeds over medium-high heat until seeds turn a golden color about 2 – 3 minutes, being careful not to burn. Toasting intensifies the flavor.

  2. Sesame seeds and poppy seeds tend to go rancid very quickly. Store them in the refrigerator 6 months or freeze up to 2 years.

◆ **Shallots** look like a cross between garlic and yellow onions. Buy shallots that are tight, with papery-looking skins and no green sprouts. They are mild and are used to season foods in which onions would be too strong. Substitute an equal amount of scallions. Store in a cool, dry place for weeks.

◆ **1.** To peel **shrimp:** pull tail off. Grasp legs and peel shell up the side removing entire hard, outer covering.

2. To **devein shrimp:** slice the back curve of the shrimp with a small paring knife. Pull out the gritty-looking black vein with the knife or your fingers; rinse under cold water. Or before peeling, grasp the end of the black vein at the head end of shrimp with the tip of a small paring knife and gently but firmly pull it out.

3. Shrimp is very perishable and must be eaten within 24 hours of purchasing. When buying shrimp, check to make sure it has no odor. Keep shrimp in a plastic bag surrounded by ice packs in the refrigerator or freeze up to 2 months. The best method for freezing is to completely submerge shrimp in water and freeze in an ice block. Thaw in the refrigerator or under cold running water.

◆ Draining off any accumulated liquid in **sour cream** carton makes the sour cream thicker and creamier.

◆ Triple washed **<u>spinach</u>** in bags is a great convenience food. Use it directly from the bag but before serving remove any stems or large ribs from the leaves. To store spinach, leaves should be very dry and should be kept in a tightly sealed bag or plastic container with as much air removed as possible.

◆ Buy **<u>strawberries</u>** that are shiny and deep red with no visible decay or moldy spots. Green cap (leaves) should be flat. To store: leave in original container and enclose tightly in a plastic bag, removing as much air as possible. Place in the coldest part of your refrigerator (back, bottom shelf). If bought fresh, will keep for several days to a week. Wash strawberries before removing the cap under cold running water. Never submerge berries in water: they absorb water like a sponge. Wash right before using: storing damp berries hastens decaying.

◆ **<u>Superfine sugar</u>** has very fine crystals and dissolves quickly. Do not confuse it with powdered sugar.

- 1. **Sweet potatoes** spoil rapidly. Store in a cool, dry place but do not refrigerate. Storing them in the cold will cause them to develop a hard core and an "off" taste.

  2. **Canned sweet potatoes** can be substituted for fresh. Three medium sweet potatoes are generally equivalent to one 16-ounce can or 2 cups mashed.

- **Thyme and rosemary** are woody herbs. Strip and chop the green leaves off the woody stems.

- **Tomatillos** look like small green tomatoes wrapped in a papery skin. They have a tart, lemony, herbal flavor. Most grocery stores carry them in the fresh produce department.

- Buy **tomatoes** that are firm, but yield to gentle pressure and are deep red. A ripe tomato should smell like a garden. Tomatoes should be stored on your counter and not in the refrigerator. Cold temperature robs tomatoes of some of their flavor. Tomatoes should last 3 – 5 days at room temperature.

- Small quantities of **<u>tomato paste</u>** can be purchased in tubes in the tomato paste aisle of the grocery store. Or freeze remaining tomato paste from the can in 1 tablespoon increments on a flat sheet; transfer to a zip top plastic bag and store in the freezer up to 3 months.

- **<u>Vinegar:</u>** If stored for a long period of time, you may notice the **"<u>mother</u>,"** or a stringy, slimy substance on the surface or floating in the vinegar. It is composed of yeast cells and various bacteria that form on the surface of fermenting liquid turning it into vinegar. <u>It is not harmful</u> and the vinegar is not spoiled. Just strain it out and use it to make your own vinegar from wine or cider.

- For **<u>vinaigrette:</u>** whisk together vinegar and spices or sugar until dissolved. Salt, sugar and spices will become suspended in the oil if not dissolved in vinegar first. Slowly whisk oil in a fine stream to incorporate thoroughly (or use a blender).

- Cook with an inexpensive **<u>wine</u>** that you would drink. Cooking wine found in the vinegar section of the grocery store is poor quality and high in sodium.

- To extend the shelf life of dry **yeast** store unopened packages in the freezer.

- The perfect place for **yeast bread** to rise is in a cold oven over a pan of hot water placed on the bottom rack.

- To **zest** a lemon, lime or orange: wash fruit well in hot water. Before cutting or juicing, remove zest (the very outermost layer of the fruit—the thin, colored part, avoiding the white pith which is bitter) with the finest part of a grater, or by peeling with a vegetable peeler and finely chopping with a knife or remove zest with a special tool called a zester.

Diva's Fast Cocktail Party Tips

- Plan 8 – 10 bites per person for 2 – 3 hour cocktail party.

- Supplement bites with pâtés, nuts, spreads or cheeses.

- Balance colors, textures, temperatures and complexity of dishes served; always include at least a couple vegetarian dishes.

- Serve bite-size individual desserts.

- Provide at least 3 paper napkins per guest to accommodate for appetizers, drinks and dessert.

- Provide 2 forks, 2 plates and 2 glasses per guest.

Diva's Fast Dinner Party Tips

- ◆ Limit appetizers to 2 – 3 bites per guest.

- ◆ Quantities to serve:

  1. Meat, Poultry, Fish per person:
     4 – 6 ounces boneless (uncooked weight)
     6 – 8 ounces bone-in (uncooked weight)

  2. Vegetables or Fruit per person: ½ cup cooked or ¼ pound uncooked

  3. Cooked Pasta or Rice per person:
     ½ cup for a side dish
     1 cup as a main dish

  4. Tossed Salad per person: 1 – 1½ cups (1 – 2 ounces)

- ◆ Always make 2 – 3 servings extra to accommodate hearty appetites
  or unexpected guests.

Diva's Fast Bar Tips

Of course there are many variables that will affect the amount of beverages that you will serve at your next get-together such as the occasion for celebration, how much your guests typically drink, or the length of the party. There are no hard and fast rules only guidelines:

◆ Plan 1 – 1½ drinks per person per hour.

◆ Buy 1 – 2 pounds of ice per person (amount depends on the temperature outside and whether ice will be used as a coolant for bottles).

◆ Provide an interesting selection of non-alcoholic drinks for your guests (for designated drivers and nondrinkers).

◆ Always have bottled water available.

Diva's Fast Bar Facts

- ◆ A 750 ml bottle of wine (3 cups) yields 4-5 servings

- ◆ A 750 ml bottle of liquor yields 17 (1½ ounce) shots

- ◆ One liter bottle of liquor yields 22 (1½ ounce) shots

- ◆ A gallon of punch yields 20 – 24 (6-ounce) servings

- ◆ One liter of soda, tonic or drink mix fills 6 – 7 (12 ounce) glasses (with ice and a shot of liquor)

- ◆ 5 pounds of ice fills 20 (12 ounce) glasses

Diva's Sample Party Bar For 10 *(adjust to any number of guests)*

- Assorted bottles of liquor

- Four 750 ml bottles of white wine

- Two 750 ml bottles of red wine

- 12 cans or bottles of beer

- 2 liters of lemon-lime soda

- 2 liters of cola

- 1 liter ginger ale

- 2 liters tonic water

- 2 liters club soda

- 2 quarts orange juice

- 1 quart Bloody Mary mix

- Garnishes (lemons, limes, cherries, olives)

- 15 – 20 pounds ice

- Twelve 16-ounce bottles of water

Diva's Fast Coffee Tips

Here are some coffee house secrets for the best-tasting coffee

◆ Start with a very clean pot—Sounds simple, but most people just rinse the pot. Coffee has an oily residue that sticks in pots and filter baskets

◆ For the best flavor use freshly ground beans and fresh cold, filtered water (1½ – 2 tablespoons per ¾ cup water)

◆ Brew just before serving; heat destroys the flavor of coffee if left on the burner too long

◆ Never reheat; coffee will become very bitter

Diva's Coffee Bar Tips

Set up a coffee bar at your next party and let your guests make their own flavored coffees.

- Offer regular and/or decaf (rent a big urn(s) for a large party, if necessary)
- Sugar Cubes (less messy than spoonable sugar)
- Sugar Substitute packets
- Creamer (cream, milk or flavored creamers from the dairy case)
- Cinnamon Sticks (for stirring) or cinnamon sugar in a shaker
- Chocolate Shavings
- Whipped Cream
- Flavorings (choose all or any)

    Kahlúa (or any coffee-flavored liqueur), Grand Marnier® (or any orange-flavored liqueur), Frangelica (hazelnut flavor), Brandy, Irish Whiskey

- Cups or Mugs
- Spoons or stirrers

Fish Fast Facts

◆ Make fish the last purchase on your list before returning home. Be prepared to keep it cold by surrounding the fish with a bag of ice. (Most fish counters or fish mongers will provide the ice if requested.)

◆ Store fish in the refrigerator up to 1 day surrounded by packs of ice. (Keep ice in tightly sealed plastic bags to prevent fish from becoming soggy.)

◆ Thaw frozen fish in the refrigerator and not at room temperature. To quickly thaw, run fish under cold water and pat dry.

◆ Serve: 4-6 ounce fillets per person
                6-8 ounce steaks per person
                12-16 ounce whole fish per person

◆ Leftover, cooked fish can be refrigerated 2-3 days. Creatively use these leftovers in omelets, salads, or soups.

Diva's Cooking With Wine Facts

◆ Wine has three main uses in the kitchen—as a marinade ingredient, as a cooking liquid, and as a flavoring in a finished dish.

◆ The function of wine in cooking is to intensify, enhance and accent the flavor and aroma of food—not to mask the flavor of what you are cooking but rather to fortify it.

◆ As with any seasoning used in cooking, care should be taken in the amount of wine used—too little is inconsequential and too much will be overpowering. Neither extreme is desirable. A small quantity of wine will enhance the flavor of the dish. Wine is known to release flavors from food that otherwise could not be experienced.

Diva's Pairing Wine With Cooking

There are exceptions to these pairings. Until you become comfortable with cooking with wine, these are simple guidelines to follow.

SUGGESTED TYPE OF WINE—TYPES OF RECIPES

Young, full bodied red wine—Red meat, red meat dishes

Young, full bodied, robust red wine—Red sauces

Earthy red, full bodied red wine—Soups with root vegetables and/or beef stock

Dry white wine or dry fortified wine— Fish/shellfish/seafood, poultry, pork, veal

Dry white wine or dry fortified wine—Light/cream sauces

Crisp, dry white wine—Seafood soups, bouillabaisse

Sweet white wine or sweet fortified wine—Sweet desserts

Dry, fortified wine (i.e.: sherry)—Consommé, poultry, vegetable soups

Regional cuisine—Regional wine

Diva's Simple Wine Ideas

Here are some simple ideas for incorporating wine into your recipes.

- When a recipe calls for water, replace some of the water with a favorite wine.

- Add a light, dry white wine to melted butter and baste grilled, broiled, or baked fish

- Stir in 1 to 2 tablespoons of a full-bodied red into brown gravy. Let simmer to create rich brown gravy for red meat.

- Mix wine with your favorite oil to baste meat and poultry.

- Freeze leftover drinking wine in ice cube trays for future cooking use.

- Serve the same wine with dinner that you used in your recipe; they will balance each other.

- If you prefer to use a fine wine during dinner, cook within the same wine family.

Substitution Chart

Substitutions or Equivalents

Yikes! You start preparing your favorite recipe, discover you are missing one ingredient and don't have time to run to the store. Here is a list of emergency substitutions. Since each ingredient has a specific function, don't expect the same results when using a suggested substitute. Some may perform the same; others may have similar properties, but may not yield exact results. Just use these suggestions for emergencies or when you don't mind a slight change in the taste or appearance of the finished product. For example when you substitute honey for sugar, your dessert will be sweet, but the honey will make baked goods brown more, add it's own flavor and require you to decrease the amount of liquid in your recipe.

ITEM	AMOUNT	SUBSTITUTION or EQUIVALENT
Allspice	1 teaspoon	= ½ teaspoon cinnamon + ⅛ teaspoon ground cloves
Apples	1 pound	= 3 or 4 medium = 3 cups sliced
Apple Pie Spice	1 teaspoon	= ½ teaspoon cinnamon + ¼ teaspoon nutmeg + ⅛ teaspoon cardamom
Arrowroot, as thickener	1½ teaspoons	= 1 tablespoon flour = 1½ teaspoons cornstarch
Asparagus	1 pound	= 16 – 20 spears
Baking powder	1 teaspoon	= ¼ teaspoon baking soda + ⅝ teaspoon cream of tartar
Bananas	1 pound	= 3 or 4 medium = 1¾ cups mashed
Beans, white, dried	1 pound	= 2 cups uncooked = 6 cups cooked
Beans, green	1 pound	= 3 cups sliced

ITEM	AMOUNT	SUBSTITUTION or EQUIVALENT
Beans, kidney, dried	1 pound	= 1½ cups, uncooked = 9 cups, cooked
Blackberries	1 quart	= 1¼ pounds = 3 – 4 cups
Blueberries	1 pound	= 2 cups
Brandy (for cooking)	¼ cup	= ¼ cup apple juice or cider = ¼ cup peach or apricot nectar
Bread crumbs, dry	¼ cup	= 1 slice bread, toasted
Bread crumbs, soft	½ cup	= 1 slice bread
Broccoli	1 pound	= 2 cups
Broth, beef or chicken	1 cup	= 1 bullion cube dissolved in boiling water
Butter	½ cup	= 1 stick = 1 stick margarine

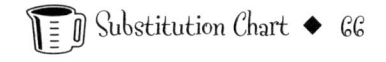

ITEM	AMOUNT	SUBSTITUTION or EQUIVALENT
Buttermilk	1 cup	= 1 cup plain yogurt = 1 cup whole or skim milk + 1 tablespoon white vinegar or lemon juice = 1 cup whole or skim milk + 1¾ teaspoons cream of tartar
Cabbage	1 pound	= 3 – 4 cups shredded = 2 cups cooked
Carrots	1 pound	= 3 cups sliced = 2½ cups shredded
Catsup	1 cup	= 1 cup tomato sauce + ¼ cup brown sugar + 2 tablespoons vinegar (for use in cooking)
Cauliflower	1 pound	= 1½ cups
Celery	1 pound	= 2 bunches
Cheese	4 ounces	= 1 cup, grated
Cherries	1 pound	= 2⅓ cups

ITEM	AMOUNT	SUBSTITUTION or EQUIVALENT
Chicken	1½ pound, boneless	1 cup cooked diced or shredded
Chili Sauce	1 cup	= 1 cup tomato sauce + ¼ cup brown sugar + 1 tablespoon vinegar + ¼ teaspoon cinnamon + dash cloves + dash allspice = 1 cup catsup + dash cloves + dash allspice
Chives, finely chopped	2 teaspoons	= 2 teaspoons finely chopped green onion tops
Chocolate Chips, semi-sweet	12 ounce bag	= 2 cups
Chocolate, semi-sweet	1 ounce square	= 1 ounce unsweetened chocolate square + 4 teaspoons sugar
Chocolate, unsweetened	1 ounce square	= 3 tablespoons cocoa plus 1 tablespoon butter or fat

ITEM	AMOUNT	SUBSTITUTION or EQUIVALENT
Cocoa	¼ cup or 4 tablespoons	= 1 ounce square unsweetened baking chocolate (decrease fat in recipe by ½ tablespoon)
Coconut	1 pound	= 5 cups shredded fresh coconut
Coconut Cream	1 cup	= 1 cup heavy or whipping cream
Coconut Milk	1 cup	= 1 cup whole or 2% milk
Coffee, ground	1 pound	= 80 tablespoons (makes 40 – 50 cups brewed coffee)
Corn	12 ears	= 2½ cups cooked kernels
Cornmeal, self-rising	1 cup	= ⅞ cup plain + 1½ teaspoons baking powder + ½ teaspoon salt
Corn Syrup	1 cup	= ⅞ cup sugar + 2 tablespoons water = ⅞ cup honey (baked goods will brown more)
Cornstarch (for thickening)	1 tablespoon	= 2 tablespoons all-purpose flour = 2 tablespoons granular tapioca
Cracker crumbs	¾ cup	= 1 cup dry bread crumbs

ITEM	AMOUNT	SUBSTITUTION or EQUIVALENT
Cranberries	1 pound	= 4 cups
Cream, heavy	1 cup	= ¾ cup milk (or canned evaporated milk) + ⅓ cup melted butter (This will not whip; for use in cooking or baking.) = 2 – 2½ cups whipped
Cream, light (half-and-half)	1 cup	= ⅞ cup milk + 3 tablespoons melted butter = 1 cup canned evaporated milk, undiluted
Cream, sour	1 cup	= ⅞ cup buttermilk or plain yogurt + 3 tablespoons melted butter
Cream, whipping	1 cup	= ⅔ cup well-chilled canned evaporated milk, whipped = 1 cup nonfat dry milk powder whipped with 1 cup ice water
Egg, raw, whole	1 large	= 3 tablespoons = 2 yolks + 1 tablespoon water (use in cookie recipes) = 2 yolks (use in custard recipes) = 2 whites as a thickening agent

ITEM	AMOUNT	SUBSTITUTION or EQUIVALENT
Egg, White	1 large	= 2 tablespoons = 2 tablespoons dry egg white powder + 2 tablespoons lukewarm water
Egg, Yolk	1 large	= 1½ tablespoons
Flour, all-purpose	1 cup, sifted	= 1 cup + 2 tablespoons cake flour = ⅝ cup potato flour = 1¼ cups rye flour = 1¼ cups coarsely ground whole-grain flour = 1 cup rolled oats, crushed = ¾ cup whole wheat flour + ¼ cup all-purpose flour
Flour, all purpose	1 pound	= 4 cups sifted = 3 cups unsifted
Flour, cake	1 cup	= 1 cup minus 2 tablespoons sifted all-purpose flour flour (⅞ cup)
Flour, cake	1 pound	= 4¾ cups

ITEM	AMOUNT	SUBSTITUTION or EQUIVALENT
Flour, self-rising	1 cup	= 1 cup all-purpose flour minus 2 tablespoons + 1½ teaspoons baking powder + ½ teaspoon salt
Garlic (fresh)	1 small clove	= ⅛ teaspoon garlic powder or instant minced garlic
Garlic Salt	1 teaspoon	= ⅛ teaspoon garlic powder + ⅞ teaspoon salt
Grapes	1 pound	= 2 cups seeded = 2½ cups seedless
Herbs, dried	1 teaspoon	= 1 tablespoon fresh herbs, minced and packed
Honey	1 cup	= 1¼ cups sugar plus ½ cup liquid (water or juice)
Horseradish	1 tablespoon, freshly grated	= 2 tablespoons bottled
Lemon, fresh	1 medium	= 1 – 3 tablespoons juice = 1 – 2 teaspoons grated peel
Lemon juice	1 teaspoon	= ½ teaspoon vinegar

ITEM	AMOUNT	SUBSTITUTION or EQUIVALENT
Lemon, juice and rind	3 tablespoons and 1 teaspoon	3 tablespoons bottled lemon juice and 1 teaspoon dried grated rind
Lemon rind, grated	1 teaspoon	= ½ teaspoon lemon extract
Lemon peel, dried	1 teaspoon	= 1 – 2 teaspoons freshly grated lemon peel = grated peel of 1 medium lemon = ½ teaspoon lemon extract

Lettuce
  Endive
  Leaf
  Romaine
	1 pound	= 5 – 6 cups shredded
		= 4½ cups
		= 5 – 6 cups
		= 6 cups

Lime	1 medium	= 1½ – 2 tablespoons juice = 1 – 1½ teaspoons grated peel
Marshmallows, miniature	1 cup	= 10 large

ITEM	AMOUNT	SUBSTITUTION or EQUIVALENT
Mayonnaise (for use in salads and salad dressings)	1 cup	= ½ cup plain yogurt + ½ cup mayonnaise = 1 cup sour cream = 1 cup cottage cheese puréed in a blender
Milk, skim	1 cup	= 1/3 cup instant nonfat dry milk + ¾ cup water
Milk, sour	1 cup	= 1 cup minus 1 tablespoon milk + 1 tablespoon vinegar or lemon juice. Stir and let stand 5 minutes.
Milk, Sweetened Condensed	1 can (1 1/3 cup)	= 1/3 cup + 2 tablespoon evaporated milk + 1 cup sugar + 3 tablespoons butter or margarine. Heat until butter and sugar are dissolved
Milk, whole	1 cup	= ½ cup canned evaporated milk + ½ cup water = 1 cup skim milk + 2 teaspoons melted butter
Mushrooms, fresh	1 pound	= 2 – 3 cups whole (depending on size and type) = 3 ounces dried = 5 cups sliced = 1 (10 ounce) can (8 ounces when drained weight)

ITEM	AMOUNT	SUBSTITUTION or EQUIVALENT
Mushrooms, canned	4 ounces	= 2 cups sliced = 6 tablespoons whole, dried mushrooms
Mustard, prepared	1 tablespoon	= 1 teaspoon dry or powdered mustard
Onion, chopped	1 small	= 1 tablespoon instant minced onion, rehydrated = 1 teaspoon onion powder; = ¼ cup frozen chopped onion
Onions	1 pound	= 3 large = 2 – 2½ cups chopped
Orange	1 medium	= $\frac{1}{3}$ – ½ cup juice = 2 – 3 tablespoons grated peel
Orange Peel, dried	1 tablespoon 2 teaspoons	= 2 – 3 tablespoons grated peel = 1 teaspoon orange extract
Parsley, fresh, chopped	1 tablespoon	= 1 teaspoon dried

ITEM	AMOUNT	SUBSTITUTION or EQUIVALENT
Peaches, Pears	1 pound	= 4 medium = 2 cups sliced
Peas, Green in pod	1 pound	= 1 cup shelled = 1 cup cooked
Peas, Black-eyed, dried	1 pound	= 2$\frac{1}{3}$ cups cooked
Pecans	1 pound	= 3$\frac{1}{2}$ cups nut meats
Plums	1 pound	= 18 – 20 whole = 2 cups halves
Potatoes, white	1 pound	= 3 medium = 2$\frac{1}{4}$ cups diced or sliced = 1$\frac{3}{4}$ cups mashed
Pumpkin Pie Spice	1 teaspoon	= $\frac{1}{2}$ teaspoon cinnamon + $\frac{1}{4}$ teaspoon ground ginger + $\frac{1}{8}$ teaspoon allspice + $\frac{1}{8}$ teaspoon nutmeg

ITEM	AMOUNT	SUBSTITUTION or EQUIVALENT
Raisins	1 pound	= 2¾ cups
Rice	1 pound	= 6 cups cooked = 2 cups uncooked = 1 cup brown rice, uncooked = 2 cups wild rice, uncooked
Shortening	1 cup	= 1⅛ cups butter (decrease salt by ⅛ teaspoon in recipe)
Sour Cream	1 cup	= 1 cup cottage cheese + ⅓ cup buttermilk + 1 tablespoon lemon juice blended until smooth = 1 cup plain yogurt = ¾ cup milk + ¾ teaspoon lemon juice + ⅓ cup butter or margarine melted, stirred
Spaghetti	1 pound	= 9 cups cooked = 4 – 5 cups (2-inch pieces)
Spinach	1 pound	= 4 cups fresh = 1½ cups cooked

ITEM	AMOUNT	SUBSTITUTION or EQUIVALENT
Squash, summer	1 pound	= 1²/₃ cups cooked and mashed
Squash, winter	1 pound	= 1 cup cooked and mashed
Strawberries	1 quart	= 4 cups sliced
Sugar, brown	1 cup 1 pound	= 1 cup granulated sugar = 2¼ cups firmly packed
Sugar, granulated	1 cup	= 1 cup firmly packed brown sugar = 1¾ cups confectioners' sugar (do not substitute in baking) = ½ cup honey = 1 cup superfine sugar = 1½ cups corn syrup = ²/₃ cup maple syrup (for last two, reduce liquid in recipe by 25 percent) = 1¹/₃ cups molasses (decrease liquid in recipe by ¹/₃ cup)
Sugar, granulated	1 pound	= 2¼ cups

ITEM	AMOUNT	SUBSTITUTION or EQUIVALENT
Sugar, powdered	1 pound	= 3¾ cups = 1 cup granulated sugar + 1 tablespoon cornstarch processed until powdery
Sweet Potatoes	1 pound	= 3 medium = 1 (16-ounce) can = 2 cups mashed
Tomatoes, canned	1 cup	= ½ cup tomato sauce plus ½ cup water = 1⅓ cups chopped fresh tomatoes, simmered
Tomatoes, fresh	1 pound	= 3 – 4 small
Tomato juice	1 cup	= ½ cup tomato sauce + ½ cup water + dash each salt and sugar = ¼ cup tomato paste + ¾ cup water + salt and sugar, to taste
Tomato Catsup	½ cup	= ½ cup tomato sauce + 2 tablespoons sugar + 1 tablespoon vinegar + ⅛ teaspoon ground cloves
Tomato Purée	1 cup	= ½ cup tomato paste + ½ cup water

ITEM	AMOUNT	SUBSTITUTION or EQUIVALENT
Tomato Soup	1 can (10¾ oz.)	= 1 cup tomato sauce plus ¼ cup water or milk
Vanilla	1-inch bean	= 1 teaspoon vanilla extract
Wine (for cooking)	½ cup	= ½ cup chicken broth = ½ cup white grape juice
Worcestershire Sauce	1 teaspoon	= 1 teaspoon bottled steak sauce
Yeast	1 cake (³/₅ oz.)	= 1 (.4 ounce) active, dry yeast package = 2¼ teaspoons active dry yeast
Yogurt, plain	1 cup	= 1 cup buttermilk = 1 cup sour cream = 1 cup cottage cheese, blended until smooth

Random Thoughts

Microwave Tips

Don't let your microwave sit like a lazy bum on your countertop. Put it to work by using these quick and easy tips:

- **<u>Soften Butter</u>** – Place cut-up butter in a microwave-safe bowl. Microwave on low power (level 1 – 3) in 20-second intervals, checking in between.

- **<u>Melt Butter</u>** – Place cut-up butter in a microwave-safe bowl. Microwave on medium power in 30-second intervals, checking in between.

- **<u>Melt Chocolate</u>** – Place chopped chocolate uncovered in a microwave-safe dish. Microwave on medium power, stirring every 20 seconds. Chocolate can be removed from oven while still lumpy; the heat of the dish and the chocolate will continue to melt lumps. Be careful not to overheat; chocolate burns at a low temperature.

Microwave Tips

- **<u>Soften Cream Cheese</u>** – Place cut-up cream cheese in a microwave-safe bowl. Microwave on high power for 15 to 20 seconds.

- **<u>Soften Ice Cream</u>** – Remove top and liner (if any) of carton. Microwave on high power in 10-second intervals, checking in between, until ice cream reaches desired consistency.

- **<u>Soften Brown Sugar</u>** – Place sugar in a microwave-safe bowl and sprinkle with a few drops of water. Cover and microwave on medium power in 30-second intervals, stirring with a fork in between, until soft.

- **<u>Warm Tortillas</u>** – Wrap tortillas in a damp paper towel or put between two plates. Microwave on high power for 40 seconds to 1 minute.

Microwave Tips

◆ **<u>Warm Maple Syrup</u>** – Place syrup in a microwave-safe measuring cup. Microwave on high power in 15-second intervals, stirring in between until desired temperature.

◆ **<u>Toast Fresh Bread Crumbs</u>** – Spread ½ cup fresh breadcrumbs on a microwave-safe plate. Microwave on high power in 1-minute intervals, tossing in between, until just golden, 2 to 3 minutes. Once crumbs start to toast, keep an eye on them; they will burn quickly.

◆ **<u>Toast Coconut</u>** – Spread ½ cup shredded coconut on a microwave-safe plate. Microwave on high power in 1-minute intervals, tossing in between, until just golden, 2 to 3 minutes.

Microwave Tips

◆ **<u>Toast Pine Nuts and Sliced Almonds</u>** – Spread nuts on a microwave-safe plate. Microwave on high power in 1-minute intervals, tossing in between, until just golden, 4 to 5 minutes.

◆ **<u>Disinfecting and Deodorizing Sponges</u>** – Don't throw out the kitchen sponge that smells like a dead fish. Soak it in water with a little added white vinegar or lemon juice then heat it on high for 1 minute. Caution! Hot, hot! Remove with tongs or a potholder. This will also disinfect any sponges you used to wipe up the juices from a raw chicken.

◆ To get the most **<u>Juice</u>** from a **<u>Lemon or Lime</u>**, microwave citrus fruits for 20 seconds before squeezing.

Microwave Tips

♦ **<u>Warm Beauty Products</u>** – Heating a hot-oil conditioning pack for your hair takes about 10 to 20 seconds and feels marvelous, as does briefly heating up a moisturizing facial mask. Caution! Stir the mask and test the temperature with your finger before applying to your face. And if hot wax hardens when you're only halfway up your calf, reheat it in the microwave.

♦ **<u>Heat serving dishes</u>** – Your food will stay much warmer if served on a preheated plate. Place the whole stack in the microwave and heat for 1 minute on high power.

Cooking in the Microwave

Cook your food about ¾ of the regular time. Stir liquids often to redistribute the heat, and always take the food out a minute or two before it's completely done, since it will continue to cook. Place veggies in a single layer (if possible) on a microwavable dish, cover tightly with plastic, and cook on high. Extra food in the microwave means added cook time. The general rule is to check for doneness every 30 seconds beyond the regular cooking time.

◆ **<u>Asparagus and Green Beans:</u>** Place 1 pound of trimmed asparagus or green beans in a microwave-safe baking dish with 1 tablespoon water. Cover and microwave on high (power level 10) until tender, 3 to 4 minutes. Immediately uncover being careful to avoid built up steam.

◆ **<u>Applesauce:</u>** In a microwave-safe bowl, place 1 pound peeled and diced apples (Macintosh, Fuji, or Gala are best) with ¼ cup water, 2 teaspoons sugar, and ¼ teaspoon cinnamon. Cover and microwave on high power until the apples are tender, 8 to 10 minutes. Mash with a fork or potato masher.

Cooking in the Microwave

- **Artichokes:** Place 2 trimmed artichokes in a deep microwave-safe baking dish with 1 tablespoon water. Cover and microwave on high (power level 10) until tender, 10 to 12 minutes.

- **Bacon:** Sandwich 6 slices of bacon between 2 double layers of paper towels. Place on a microwave-safe plate. Microwave on high power until cooked through, 3 to 5 minutes.

- **Carrots:** Place 1 pound thinly sliced carrots in a microwave-safe baking dish with 1 tablespoon water. Cover and microwave on high (power level 10) until tender, 4 to 6 minutes. Immediately uncover being careful to avoid built up steam.

Cooking in the Microwave

◆ **Corn on the Cob:** Place unshucked corn on a microwave-safe plate. Microwave on high (power level 10) for 6 minutes. Let stand for 5 minutes. Carefully remove the husks and silk.

◆ **Roasting Garlic:** It takes 45 minutes to roast garlic in the oven but less than 8 in the microwave. Slice off the top of the head to reveal all the cloves. Place the head in a small, deep dish drizzle with 2 tablespoons of olive oil. Spoon 2 tablespoons of water into the bottom of the dish, cover it with plastic wrap, and cook at medium power for 7 to 7½ minutes. Let stand for a few minutes before unwrapping.

◆ **Partially Cook Foods for the Grill:** To cut the grilling time of vegetables, cook them partway before putting them over the hot coals. Heat new potatoes for 2 minutes (prick them first), and bell peppers for 1 minute.

Cooking in the Microwave

♦ __Popcorn:__ Place ½ cup popcorn kernels in a large microwave-safe bowl with 1 tablespoon olive or canola oil. Cover with a microwave-safe plate and microwave on high power until the majority of the kernels have popped, 3 to 5 minutes.

♦ __"Baked" Potato:__ Prick a potato all over and rub with olive oil. Place on a microwave-safe plate. Microwave, uncovered, on high power until tender and easily pierced with a paring knife, about 4 – 6 minutes depending on the size. You can cook as many as will fit. For **Mashed Potatoes,** remove skin and mash. Be sure to heat the milk with the butter in the microwave before adding it.

Cooking in the Microwave

◆ **<u>Poach Salmon:</u>** Rub pieces of skinless salmon fillet with a little olive oil and season with salt and pepper; place in a shallow microwave-safe baking dish with 2 tablespoons white wine vinegar or rice vinegar (to add flavor) and enough water to reach halfway up the fish. Cover and microwave on high power until the fish is opaque throughout, 3 to 4 minutes. If the fish is not fully cooked, microwave, covered, on high in 45-second intervals. Remove from liquid and serve warm.

◆ Love **<u>S'mores?</u>** Put marshmallows in the microwave for 15 – 20 seconds and then press between graham crackers with a chocolate bar.

◆ **<u>Spinach, Mushrooms, and Snow Peas</u>** (tender veggies): Cook on high in 30-second intervals until desired doneness.

Cooking in the Microwave

◆ **<u>Winter Squash</u>:** Carefully cut washed squash in half lengthwise and scrape out the seeds. Place cut-side down in a microwave-safe baking dish. Microwave on high power until tender and easily pierced with a paring knife, 10 to 13 minutes for a medium (3-pound) butternut or spaghetti squash; 6 to 8 minutes for a medium (1½-pound) acorn squash. Let stand for 5 minutes.

Safe (Non-Food Items) for the microwave:

1. Glass and ceramic dishes

2. Paper plates, towels, and napkins

3. Wax and parchment paper

Unsafe for the microwave:

1. Aluminum foil or any metal

2. Brown paper bags

3. Disposable plastic containers
(such as margarine tubs, cottage-cheese, and yogurt cups)

4. Onetime-use plastic containers

5. Dishes with decorative metallic paint, trim or rim

6. Foam-insulated cups, bowls, plates, and trays

Dishwasher

Whoever thought of the dishwasher as a workhorse when it comes to keeping anything clean but dishes. When in doubt, wash on the top rack and turn off the heat/drying cycle. Here are a few ideas for odd items that can be washed in a dishwasher:

◆ **<u>Baby Toys</u>** – Action figures and other small washable toys can be cleaned on the top rack. But just be sure to put pieces in a mesh lingerie bag or you might be trying to dig Polly Pockets® out of the drain. This is true of any other small objects that you might want to try.

◆ **<u>Baseball caps</u>** can get beat up pretty bad in the washing machine but will hold their shape in the dishwasher. Wash on the top rack and without dirty dishes. Food will get caught in the cloth.

Dishwasher

- ◆ **<u>Ceramic cabinet knobs and pulls</u>** clean easier but keep them relegated to the silverware basket. They are a lot of work to remove, wash and replace, but the grime and fingerprints will easily and quickly be washed away.

- ◆ **<u>Plastic, aluminum or steel fan grilles, switch plates, and vent covers</u>** will come out spic and span. Never put in enameled, painted, plated or coated anything.

- ◆ **<u>Plastic Hairbrushes and combs</u>** can go for a cycle, but do not put wood or natural boar-bristle brushes in this hot, wet environment. Be sure to remove all the hair to keep the drain clear. (Okay, I have to admit that this tip kinda grosses me out a little bit!)

- ◆ Wash **<u>light-fixture globes or covers</u>** on top rack on the china or delicate cycle, but, please, not antique, enameled, or painted.

Dishwasher

- Making mashed **potatoes** for a crowd? Make your life easier by washing them on the top rack with no detergent and only the rinse-only cycle.

- **Rubber or plastic shoes** like rain boots (remove the liners and lie horizontally).

- Hang **Flip-flops** over the tines in the top rack. **Crocs are not dishwasher-safe.**

- **Sports Equipment** like shinguards, knee pads, and mouth guards get sanitized on the top rack.

- **Tools** with metal or plastic handles (not wooden) can be washed. Be sure to dry thoroughly and rub with a little lubricating oil to prevent rusting.

Dishwasher

The following sound like they should be dishwasher safe, but really aren't:

- **<u>Cast-iron pans</u>** will rust—my grandmother barely hand-washed hers.

- **<u>Enameled Cast-iron</u>** will chip and the exposed area will rust.

- **<u>Copper</u>** pots and pans dent really easily.

- **<u>China and expensive flatware</u>** can get worn with repeated washings. General rule: if you don't want to pass along to the next generation then you can. If you put sterling silver flatware in the dishwasher, don't mix it with stainless-steel. The two just don't play nice. A chemical reaction between the two metals will cause a permanent discoloration on the silver.

- **<u>Crystal glasses</u>** can get etched and will lose their characteristic smoothness; the dry cycle (heat) can cause cracks.

Dishwasher

The following sound like they should be dishwasher safe, but really aren't:

◆ The vacuum seal (the feature on **insulated glasses and containers**) can be damaged with water seepage.

◆ All **knives** (including steak knives) will get dull. The abrasive washing powder or liquid will take away the sharp edge. Always hand wash. My pet peeve is ruining knives in the dishwasher.

◆ The hot water and high heat can warp and dry out **wooden cutting boards** causing them not to lay flat leaving them essentially useless.

◆ **Wooden spoons** can crack and warp. If you don't mind replacing them often, throw them in.

Make other small appliances multifunctional as well:

Ice Cream Maker

◆ **Make frozen hot chocolate.** Prepare instant hot chocolate according to the package directions, then pour it into the machine and freeze for about 20 minutes.

◆ **Make margaritas.** Mix all the ingredients from your favorite recipe (excluding the alcohol which will prevent freezing) into the ice cream maker. When the liquid has frozen, add the tequila and triple sec.

◆ **Make Slurpees:** Set up the machine according to the manufacturer's directions. Pour in 1½ cups of any beverage (cola, kool-ade, fruit juice) and start the machine. A thick slush will form after 10 to 15 minutes; scoop it into glasses and serve. Makes two servings.

Rice Cooker

- **Make hot cereal.** Even though it takes twice as long, the cereal is smoother and creamier than the stovetop version.

- **Spa time.** Steam towels to offer guests before dinner. Dampen several washcloths. Fold or roll until small enough to fit inside the steamer. Steam until hot; remove with tongs and place on a tray or plate. You can also use these towels for a facial.

Waffle Iron

- **Make grilled cheese.** I think I use mine more for sandwiches than for waffles. Butter one side of two pieces of bread. Place one bread on waffle iron buttered side down. Place a slice of your choice of cheese and top with the other buttered bread with the butter on the outside. Close grill and cook until cheese is oozy and melted and bread is toasted.

Double Duty

Here are some uncommon suggestions for some common household items. Experiment to get the best results.

◆ **<u>Baby oil</u>:** Apply a small amount to a cotton cloth and shine chrome fixtures (faucets) in the bathroom. Also adds a shine to hubcaps.

◆ **<u>Car wax</u>:** Apply a thin layer to a stovetop (not the burners) and then wipe off. Spills will then easily wipe off. Also wax toilet tanks and smooth bathroom tiles (avoiding the grout and tiled floors) for a pristine shine that repels stains.

◆ **<u>Catsup</u>:** Renew the color and luster of copper. Rub an ample amount on copper cookware and let it stand for 5 minutes. Rinse off with hot water and towel dry to discover an incredible shine.

◆ **<u>Coffee filter</u>:**

1. Fit the filter over the opening of a glass or small jar and secure with a rubber band, then pour in some yogurt (or sour cream). Any liquid from the yogurt will drain through the filter leaving behind a thicker and creamier yogurt (or sour cream).

2. Use as a "drip catcher". Just slide the wooden stick of frozen Popsicles or ice creams through the center of the filter to keep hands mess free.

3. Use as a flower-pot liner: put a filter in the bottom of a small pot when repotting before filling with soil.

4. Use as a protective cover in the microwave over a bowl or a plate to prevent splattering.

5. Place between fragile dishes to prevent scratches or dings.

◆ **<u>Colander</u>:** Invert over your tray of burgers or hot dogs to use as a bug tent during a cookout.

◆ **<u>Comb</u>:** Use as a carpet rake to fluff up a spot squashed by a furniture leg.

◆ **Dryer sheets:**

1. Will remove the gunk form the soleplate of an iron. Just rub a warm iron over the dryer sheet until the residue disappears and all that remains is a pristine iron. Now you have no excuses for not ironing.

2. Used dryer sheets make excellent cloths for dusting your furniture.

3. Soak a dryer sheet in warm water in a pot to loosen cooked on or burnt food.

4. Scrub the tough soap scum build up off shower doors with a dampened used dryer sheet.

◆ **Egg slicer:** In addition to eggs, slice mushrooms, strawberries and fresh mozzarella cheese balls into equal pieces.

◆ **Flat iron:** Recycle your ribbons and bows tied around your presents by running them thru your flat iron. Removes the telltale creases and wrinkles.

◆ <u>Fork</u>:

1. Use the tines of a fork or the tip of a sharp knife to poke a small hole in the foil seals of vegetable oil or pancake syrup to control the amount they pour.

2. Use to gently fluff carpet to its original height by removing dents left by heavy furniture.

◆ **<u>Envelopes</u>:** Cut the end off a corner to make a good funnel for filling salt and pepper shakers or use to refill pepper grinders with peppercorns.

◆ <u>Felt circles</u>:

1. Attach a circle to both sides of a clothes hanger to prevent clothes from slipping off.

2. Fasten a felt to each of the four corners of a picture frame to prevent marring of painted walls.

◆ **<u>Gift Box</u>:** Assemble the box and cut X's in the top to use as a cupcake carrier to stabilize your yummy payload.

- **Grocery bags:** Save money on trash bags by reusing plastic grocery bags by lining small trash cans. To keep them from slipping down, affix a plastic, self-adhesive hook to both sides of the outside of the trash can. Hang the shopping bag handles from the hooks.

- **Hair dryer:** Hot air will quickly loosen price labels or stickers.

- **Hairspray:** A quick spritz will banish static cling in the wintertime.

- **Hair conditioner:** Use as a substitute for shaving gel. Softens the skin as well.

- **Ice cube trays:** Use as an organizational tool by storing thumb tacks, paper clips, sewing notions, earrings, rings or other small items or jewelry.

- **Ketchup bottle:** Empty, wash, and fill with pancake batter. Portion with precision control to make baby pancakes or shapes without the usual mess.

- **<u>Kitchen shears:</u>** Easily chop canned veggies (like tomatoes) in the can using a cutting motion.

- **<u>Kool-aid</u>®:** Use this kids' drink as a dishwasher stain remover (lime and rust) from the inside walls. Pour 1 packet lemonade drink mix (which contains citric acid or citric acid crystals) into the detergent cup and then run a regular cycle in an empty dishwasher. Repeat as necessary.

- **<u>Lemon/lime soda:</u>** Soak or coat apple slices with Sprite® or 7-Up® to prevent browning. Kids prefer this method over the traditional lemon juice and water.

- **<u>Milk:</u>** Soak frozen fish in milk overnight to eliminate any fishy or frostbitten taste.

- **<u>Muffin tin:</u>** Overturn and use as a cooling rack for hot pans right from the oven. The space between the cups allows cool air to move freely.

- **<u>Mustard or Soy Sauce packets:</u>** Use these condiments from take-out as mini ice packs for small boo-boos. Just pop them in the freezer and use on your next mishap.

◆ **<u>Name tags</u>:**

1. Jot the name and attach to your guest's coat at your party to quickly retrieve it at the end.

2. Use as an address label on a large envelope.

◆ **<u>Newspaper plastic bags</u>:** Slip over a wet umbrella to protect your car or carpet from dripping water or to store in your purse when shopping.

◆ **<u>Paint brush</u>:** A dry paintbrush (with bristles at least 3 inches long) is great for dusting both the surface and grooves of your collectibles. Use a pastry brush from the kitchen which is softer than a paintbrush to dust framed photos and is easier to dip into corners and places that are difficult to reach.

◆ **<u>Cheap Paper plates</u>:**

1. Use as a lid over dishes in the microwave to prevent splatters.

2. Measure dry ingredients onto a plate and pour into the mixing bowl.

◆ **Post It® Notes:** Run the sticky side between computer keys to collect crumbs, lint and dust.

◆ **Rubber bands:**

1. When a jar is hard to open, wrap several rubber bands around the lid to give a better grip.

2. Wrap the ends of plastic hangers to prevent slippery garments such as sundresses, camisoles, slips, etc. from slipping off.

◆ **Rubber gloves:** Don a pair of damp rubber dishwashing gloves and run your hand over upholstery covered with pet hair. The hair will cling to the gloves. Rinse under running water to remove the hair.

◆ **Rubbing alcohol:** Remove ball point pen ink from clothing by dabbing with a clean white cloth moistened with little alcohol. Also removes permanent marker from washable surfaces such as countertops and walls.

- **Soap case:** Protect your camera when you travel by storing in a hard plastic soap case to keep it safe in your carry-on bag.

- **Tape:**

1. For a smoother lips, press the sticky side to your lips to remove dry skin (that is not cracked) before applying lipstick.

2. Put a small piece of tape where the nail will go when hanging a picture on a plaster wall. This will prevent the plaster from chipping when you hammer in the nail.

- **Telephone cord:** Wrangle and untangle unruly wires behind TV's or computers by wrapping a spiral telephone cord around the wires. Use different color cords to differentiate which appliance the wires belong to; i.e. black for TV, white for computer.

- **<u>Tennis ball:</u>** Use a new tennis ball to scrub scuff marks off tile, vinyl, woodwork and even painted walls. It won't harm the surface.

- **<u>Toilet brush:</u>** Use a new, unused toilet brush to freshen your Garbage Disposal: Sprinkle baking soda in it along with a few drops dishwashing liquid. Scrub with the brush, getting under the rubber gasket and all around the inside. Then, turn on water and let the disposal run to flush thoroughly. For a fresh citrus scent, throw in a few cut up lemons or limes and run them through, too, using lots of water.

- **<u>Toothpaste:</u>** Use to restore damaged CD's. Apply a dot of non-gel toothpaste to a soft cloth and rub in a straight line from the center outward over any scratches. Rinse with cool water.

- **<u>Uncooked spaghetti:</u>** Test baked goods to see if they are done. Poke a strand in the center; if it comes out clean your goodie is finished cooking.

◆ <u>Velcro</u>®:

1. Stick pieces to the floor and the bottom of the rug to keep in place and prevent bunching.

2. Place on chair pads and chair seats to prevent cushions from sliding off the chairs.

3. Never lose the remote again. Attach a piece to the remote and side of the TV.

4. Remove pills from favorite sweaters with the loop side to get rid of those pesky balls.

◆ **<u>WD-40</u>®:** Removes crayon marks from clothes and walls: Spray with WD-40®, then gently wipe, using a paper towel or clean cloth. If the mark is stubborn, sprinkle a little baking soda on a damp sponge and gently rub in a circular motion. If the WD-40® leaves a residue, gently wipe off with a sponge soaked in soapy water; rinse clean; blot dry. Another method is to use a hair dryer—it heats the wax and wipes away instantly. If the color remains, like red usually does, wet a cloth with bleach and wipe.

◆ **Wine bottles:**

1. In a pinch, use as a rolling pin to flatten pie crust or pizza dough.

2. Keep tall boots in shape and upright in your closet.

◆ **Wine corks:** Slip one or two corks under a pot lid's handle to have something safe to grab when you don't want to use a potholder.

◆ **Ziploc® plastic bags:**

1. Avoid embarrassment at the airport when security checks your travel bag by packing undies and bras in separate large Ziploc® bags.

2. Snip off a corner and use as a pastry bag to pipe frosting onto your favorite dessert.

Green Cleaners

These homemade cleaners are more economical and safer to use than commercial brands. Be sure to label each bottle carefully and make only as much as you need for each job.

◆ <u>Anti-Bacterial Cleaner</u>:

1. Mix 2 cups distilled water, 3 tablespoons castile soap and 20 – 30 drops tea tree oil. Use like Lysol® brand to clean toys, hands, toilets or in the laundry.

2. Or mix ¾ cup chlorine bleach with enough warm distilled water and 1 tablespoon laundry detergent. Use gloves when using.

3. Or make a $^{50}/_{50}$ mixture of hydrogen peroxide with distilled water. Use this solution to disinfect countertops, cutting boards or sinks. Fill a bottle, spray surfaces and wipe with a clean, dry cloth.

◆ <u>Dishwasher soap</u>: Mix equal parts borax and washing soda. Increase the amount of washing soda for hard water. Store in an airtight container.

- **Disinfectant:** Vigorously mix 2 teaspoons borax, 4 tablespoons white vinegar in 3 cups hot water. To make it stronger add 1 tablespoon castile soap.

- <u>**Granite countertop cleaner:**</u> Mix ¾ cup rubbing alcohol with 5 – 6 drops dishwashing liquid. Place in a spray bottle and clean with a micro fiber towel.

- <u>**Laundry Detergent:**</u> Mix 1 cup Ivory Soap (Fels Naptha Soap) with ½ cup washing soda and ½ cup borax. Use 1 tablespoon for light loads and 2 tablespoons for heavy loads. Since every washing machine is different, adjust the amounts as necessary.

- <u>**Multi-Purpose Deep Cleaner**</u>: Thoroughly mix 1-cup sudsy ammonia, with ½ cup white vinegar, ¼ cup baking soda and enough warm water to make 1 gallon. Stir or shake well to thoroughly mix. Use on most washable surfaces excluding wood and granite. Makes your porcelain sparkle!

◆ **<u>Room Deodorizer:</u>**

1. For strong smells in the kitchen, boil white vinegar while cooking.

2. Or set a dish of white vinegar or lemon juice in the room with the odor.

3. Or mix 1 cup water, 1 teaspoon ground cinnamon and 1 teaspoon ground cloves. Bring to a boil in the microwave or on the stovetop. Set near the offensive odor.

◆ **<u>Soft Scrub:</u>** Mix 2 tablespoons baking soda with enough castile soap to make a creamy mixture.

◆ **<u>Wallpaper Remover:</u>** Mix equal parts white vinegar and hot water. Apply with a sponge or spray a light mist over the paper. Let sit until the adhesive is softened. Repeat as necessary. Paper may be peeled away or gently scraped clean.

◆ **Wipes**: Use Bounty® or Viva® select-a-size paper towels. Cut the roll in half (an electric or serrated knife works best for this) and remove the center cardboard roll. Find a plastic container the same size as the ½ roll with a tight-fitting lid. Poke, drill or cut a slit in the center of the lid. Pour the mixture over towels and let absorb. Start the towels by pulling out the first wipe from the center of the roll and feed through the slit.

1. **Face Wipes:** To remove makeup — Mix 2 tablespoons liquid baby bath/wash with 2 cups water.

2. **Bathroom Wipes:** Mix 1 cup Pine cleaner with 1 cup water.

3. **Bug Wipes:** Mix 1 cup Avon Skin-So-Soft® with 1 cup water.

4. **Window Wipes:** Mix 1½ cups glass cleaner and ½ cup water.

5. **Disinfectant Wipes:**

   1. Mix 1 cup hydrogen peroxide with 1 cup distilled water.

   2. Or Mix ½ cup of your favorite anti-bacterial cleaner (like Mr. Clean®) with 1½ cups water.

◆ **<u>Bathroom Faucets, sinks and tubs</u>:** To remove lime deposits rub the cut side of a lemon on the lime scale and let sit for several minutes. Wipe clean with a wet cloth. Repeat for heavy scale. You may also squeeze lemon juice and scrub with an old toothbrush. Polish with a dry cloth.

◆ **<u>Candle Wax</u>:**

1. To remove wax from carpeting or other fabric, first scrape away any excess. Then, place a brown paper bag over the wax and run a warm iron over the bag. The wax will melt right into the bag! Continue moving the bag around as you pick up the wax so you are always using a clean section. If a little grease stain remains on carpet, sprinkle with baking soda and allow to sit overnight before vacuuming, which will remove the grease residue. If colored wax leaves a stain on carpet, blot with spot remover or carpet cleaner, following label directions.

2. Prevent melted candle wax from sticking inside votive holders by spraying the inside with a thin coating of nonstick cooking spray before popping in the tea light. After the candle burns down, the remaining wax will slip out.

3. To prevent the wax from melting and sticking to the inside of a votive candleholder, pour a bit of water in the holder, then place the candle on top. If you're reading this tip too late, and there's already wax stuck inside your candleholder, pop it in the freezer for an hour. The wax will chip right off.

◆ **Carpet Cleaner:**

1. Plain warm water can remove most soils from carpet. Blot with a clean, white cloth.

2. For stubborn stains, mix equal parts white vinegar and water. Blot (not rub) with this mixture until stain disappears.

3. To aid your vacuum in cleaning pet hairs, run a dampened sponge mop over carpet. The fur/hair will ball up and be easier to remove.

3. Baby wipes are miracle-workers on carpet stains, from motor oil to blood, they remove almost anything!

4. **Permanent Marker on Carpet:** Dab a washcloth soaked in rubbing alcohol onto the marker stain. Do not rub it—just blot it—rotating the cloth to a clean spot every time.

- **Cast Iron Pans:** To gently and effectively clean your cast iron skillets after most uses, wipe out excess food with a dry paper towel, then sprinkle salt inside the pan. Wipe clean with a clean, dry paper towel. The salt acts as an abrasive to scratch off any stuck-on particles of food without using soap and water, which can remove your seasoning. For stubborn stuck-on food, use a putty knife to scrape it off. You may, however, need to re-season the pan after scraping.

- **Cloudy Drinking Glasses:** Soak them for an hour or longer in slightly warm white vinegar. Then, use a nylon-net or plastic dish scrubber to remove film. Still there? The damage may be etching (tiny scratches that occur in the dishwasher) and is permanent, sorry to say. To avoid this altogether, hand-wash your best glasses.

- **Copper Pans:** Rub the bottom of copper pans with used lemon rinds dipped in salt.

◆ **<u>Dishwasher:</u>** Run 1½ cups white vinegar through a wash cycle in your dishwasher to keep it clean and fresh.

◆ **<u>Drain Cleaner:</u>**

1. For light clogs heat (don't boil) ½-cup table salt in 1-gallon water and pour down the drain.

2. To make a stronger cleaner, pour ½-cup baking soda down the drain followed by ½ cup white vinegar. Wait 15 minutes and pour boiling water down the drain to clear the residue. (This chemical reaction breaks down fatty acids creating soap and glycerin allowing the clog to wash down the drain.) Caution: only use this method with metal plumbing. Use hot water, not boiling, for plastic pipes.

◆ **<u>Furniture:</u>**

1. To make furniture polish, mix 1-cup vegetable oil and ½ cup lemon juice. Shake well and apply with a soft cloth.

- **Furniture:**

2. Or Mix 4 drops lemon oil with ½-cup warm water.

3. Remove water spots or rings apply toothpaste or mayonnaise with a damp cloth and rub into the spot or ring. Once it is removed buff with a furniture polish.

- **Garbage Disposal Cleaner:** To get rid of smells, feed frozen vinegar cubes (freeze in an ice cube tray) down the disposal. After grinding, rinse by running cold water through the drain.

- **Grease or Oil Spills:** Cover with baking soda or kitty litter to absorb then sweep up. To remove stains, add more baking soda and scrub with a wet brush.

- **Ink Stains:** The best way to get out ink stains is to put rubbing alcohol on the stain—it disappears! But must be done before washing.

- **<u>Linoleum or Vinyl Floor Cleaner</u>:**

1. Clean with plain club soda.

2. Make a solution of 1 cup white vinegar plus 4 drops of Baby Oil in gallon of warm water. For tough jobs add ¼-cup borax. Shake or stir vigorously.

- **<u>Microwave Cleaner</u>:** Stir 2 tablespoons of baking soda or freshly squeezed lemon juice in 1-cup water in a microwave-safe bowl. Boil for 5 minutes. Wipe clean.

- **<u>Mold and Mildew Cleaner</u>:** Apply full strength white vinegar or lemon juice with a sponge or scrub with a used toothbrush.

- **<u>Mothballs</u>:**

1. Use fresh cedar chips in a square of cheesecloth. Make your own by shaving a block of cedar with a planer.

2. Or place cedar oil in cotton balls.

3. Bundle lavender, rosemary, vitiver, and rose petals in sachets.

- **<u>Photos Stuck Together</u>:** With a hair dryer on low, slowly melt them apart.

- **<u>Rust Remover</u>:** Make a paste of salt and lime juice. Leave mixture on 2 – 3 hours. Use the lime rind as a scrubber.

- **<u>Smelly Shoes</u>:** Simply fill a tube sock with kitty litter, baking soda, or tea leaves and tie the end closed; place the filled socks in the shoes when you're not wearing them. These sachets can be used over and over in any kind of shoe.

- **<u>Stainless Steel</u>:**

1. Clean fingerprints and grime with a cloth dampened with undiluted white vinegar.

2. To make your appliances shine, make a mixture of 1 cup rubbing alcohol and 1 or 2 tablespoons baby oil. Thoroughly mix and apply with a soft cloth.

- **<u>Tarnished Silverware</u>:** Line a pan with aluminum foil. Fill with water heated to 150 degrees and add 1 tablespoon baking soda and 1 teaspoon salt per 2 cups of water. Lay silverware in pan, touching aluminum foil. Watch the tarnish disappear!

◆ **<u>Tile, Stone or Brick Floor:</u>** Mix 1 cup white vinegar with enough warm water to make 1 gallon. Rinse with clear water.

◆ **<u>Tub and Tile Cleaner:</u>** Wipe surfaces with white vinegar then scour surfaces with baking soda. Rinse with clear water.

◆ **<u>Veggie Wash:</u>**

1. Mix 1 tablespoon baking soda with 1 tablespoon Fruit Fresh® (citrus acid) in 1 gallon water. Soak grapes and veggies (except leafy greens) in this water for a few minutes; use a vegetable scrubber for smooth veggies. For grapes, after soaking, swish in the mixture. Rinse thoroughly and pat dry with a towel or let air-dry.

2. To remove the wax from fruits and vegetables, wet the skin and sprinkle with baking soda. Rub all over; rinse well and dry with a towel. Use this method just before cooking or serving.

- **<u>Wayward Paint</u>:** Protect doorknobs and hardware in the kitchen and bathroom when you're painting by wrapping foil around them to catch any drips. The foil molds to the shape of whatever it's covering and stays firmly in place until the job is complete.

- **<u>White Heat Marks and Water Rings on Wood Furniture</u>:** If the wood has a good finish (don't try on bare wood), mix equal parts of baking soda and regular white, non-gel toothpaste. Lightly dampen corner of a clean, soft white cloth with water and dip into the paste. With circular motion gently buff the marks for a few minutes. Wipe area clean, and buff to a shine. Follow with furniture polish. (If rings remain after buffing five minutes or so, they may have penetrated the wood; you might have to refinish the piece). If that doesn't work, dip a cloth in vegetable oil, then in cigarette ashes, then rub it over the mark. Another method is to rub real mayonnaise onto the stain, allow to sit overnight, then wipe with a dry towel.

◆ **Window Cleaner:**

1. Mix 1 pint rubbing alcohol with 2 tablespoons sudsy ammonia, 1 teaspoon dishwashing liquid, and a couple drops blue food coloring in a gallon jug. Fill with distilled water. Label jug with a permanent marker. Fill spray bottles as needed and use like the national brand.

2. **Outdoor window cleaner:** Mix 3 tablespoons liquid dishwashing soap with 1-tablespoon dishwasher anti-spotting agent (like Jet Dry®). Put soap and anti-spotting agent into a spray bottle attachment for your garden hose. Spray upper windows and let them dry. This mixture is for cleaning the higher windows on your house that can't be reached except with a ladder.

◆ **Wood Floors:**

1. Make a cleaner by combining ½ cup white vinegar, 2 tablespoons vegetable oil and 15 drops peppermint oil. Shake vigorously to mix well.

2. Temporarily fix scratches on wood floors by rubbing them with fine steel wool dipped in floor wax.